The Whisper of a Firefly

A Children's Book for Loss

ISBN: 978-0-692-59050-8
First edition 2015
Printed in the United States of America.
Children. Families. Loss. Signs.

THE WHISPER OF A FIREFLY/written by Kara Scheer, Fargo, N.D.

Summary: Children's book for families that encourages them to find
comfort from the signs they may see after losing a loved one.
Children can draw pictures in the book of the special person they
have lost and any signs they may have seen.

*A special thanks to Marc de Celle, Jennifer Nelson, and Leandra
Ostrom for your invaluable writing advice and help, and to all my
friends and family who have supported me in this adventure.

Written in memory of Lisa Jahnke
1965-2014
A loving mother, a cherished daughter and sister, and a devoted teacher. Lisa is greatly missed.

THE WHISPER OF A FIREFLY is a children's book about finding comfort from the special signs one may see after losing a loved one. I wanted to share some of the signs that we were blessed to experience after my sister passed away. We continue to encounter Lisa's presence in our lives every day.

I hope that this book will bring comfort to you and your family as you watch for signs from someone that you have lost. Thank you to all who have given love and support to my family and I. Also, a big Thank You to Steph for bringing this book to life.
Ashlyn, Amanda, Soren, Sawyer, and Areya always keep watching for your signs.

Kara Scheer
November 2015

When you lose someone so dear, someone important to you, it's okay to be angry and feel that it's not fair.

Believe in your heart that the special person you miss is now an angel watching over you, hearing you through a wish, or a prayer.

When you lose someone so dear, watch for signs that give you comfort in knowing your loved one is near.

Beautiful signs that tell us, "I'm still here." Some of these may be subtle, whereas others are crystal clear.

When you lose someone so dear, you may see signs day or night. Some may be small while others are big and bright.

This could be a single firefly visiting you at night, shining and flashing its beautiful light.

When you lose someone so dear, signs can give you a special peace of mind.

These may be the simplest of kinds, such as perfectly placed flowers, just for you to find.

When you lose someone so dear, signs may come with beauty such as bluebirds will bring.

Perhaps you will see a bluebird watching you or get a special feeling when you hear one sing.

When you lose someone so dear, watch for signs as you honor them year after year.

Signs such as 48 pink balloons floating near, then heading straight up through the clouds until they disappear.

When you lose someone so dear, watch for signs everyday from critters who seem to have something to say.

This may be a dragonfly who comes to share the beautiful day, and then decides to go, or it just might stay.

When you lose someone so dear, trust that your loved one is watching over family far and near.

This might even be seen with a baby, whom makes it very clear, as she recovers from an illness, a special angel is near.

When you lose someone so dear, the stars may show you signs when the sky becomes clear.

Signs that can appear as beautiful shooting stars so bright, you'll want to stand up and cheer.

Draw pictures of a loved one that you have lost, and some of the special signs that you have seen.

Have fun drawing pictures with your family too!

www.ingramcontent.com/pod-product-compliance
Lightning Source LLC
Chambersburg PA
CBHW060755150426
42811CB00058B/1412